My School

By

Kirsty Holmes

CRABTREE
PUBLISHING COMPANY
WWW.CRABTREEBOOKS.COM

Published in Canada
Crabtree Publishing
616 Welland Avenue
St. Catharines, ON
L2M 5V6

Published in the United States
Crabtree Publishing
PMB 59051
350 Fifth Ave, 59th Floor
New York, NY 10118

Published by Crabtree Publishing Company in 2019

Author: Kirsty Holmes

Editors: Holly Duhig, Janine Deschenes

Design: Jasmine Pointer

Proofreader: Melissa Boyce

**Production coordinator and
prepress technician (interior):** Margaret Amy Salter

Prepress technician (covers): Ken Wright

Print coordinator: Katherine Berti

Photographs

All images from Shutterstock

Printed in the U.S.A./122018/CG20181005

Library and Archives Canada Cataloguing in Publication

Holmes, Kirsty, author
        My school / Kirsty Holmes.

(Our values)
Includes index.
Issued in print and electronic formats.
ISBN 978-0-7787-5424-4 (hardcover).--
ISBN 978-0-7787-5447-3 (softcover).--
ISBN 978-1-4271-2219-3 (HTML)

        1. Schools--Juvenile literature. 2. School day--Juvenile literature.
3. School environment--Juvenile literature. I. Title.

LB1513.H66 2018   j372   C2018-905487-5
                                                                      C2018-905488-3

Library of Congress Cataloging-in-Publication Data

CIP available at the Library of Congress

Contents

Words that look like **this** can be found in the glossary on page 24.

Going to School

Have you already started school? Or maybe you are getting ready for your first school day. School is a big part of your life. Most people go to school for 13 years or longer!

Library

Classmates, teachers, and staff

Cafeteria

What will I find at school?

Playground

Classroom

5

A School Community

Your school is more than a building with classrooms and hallways. It is also your classmates, your teachers, and other adults who work and **volunteer** there.

You and all of the people who learn, teach, work, and volunteer at your school are part of your school **community**.

principal

office staff

janitor

teacher

classmates

Learning at School

School is for learning. At school, you learn the things you need to know to meet your **goals**. It is a teacher's job to help you learn.

It is normal to have some challenges when you are learning something new! Ask your teacher if you need any help at school.

My Classroom

You learn in your classroom. Classrooms are shared by groups of students in the same grade. They are called classmates.

Hang your coats and backpacks on hooks in your classroom or in the hallway.

You can make your classroom a great place to learn by keeping it clean. Help clean up by putting trash where it belongs, keeping your desk tidy, and wearing indoor shoes.

Working Together

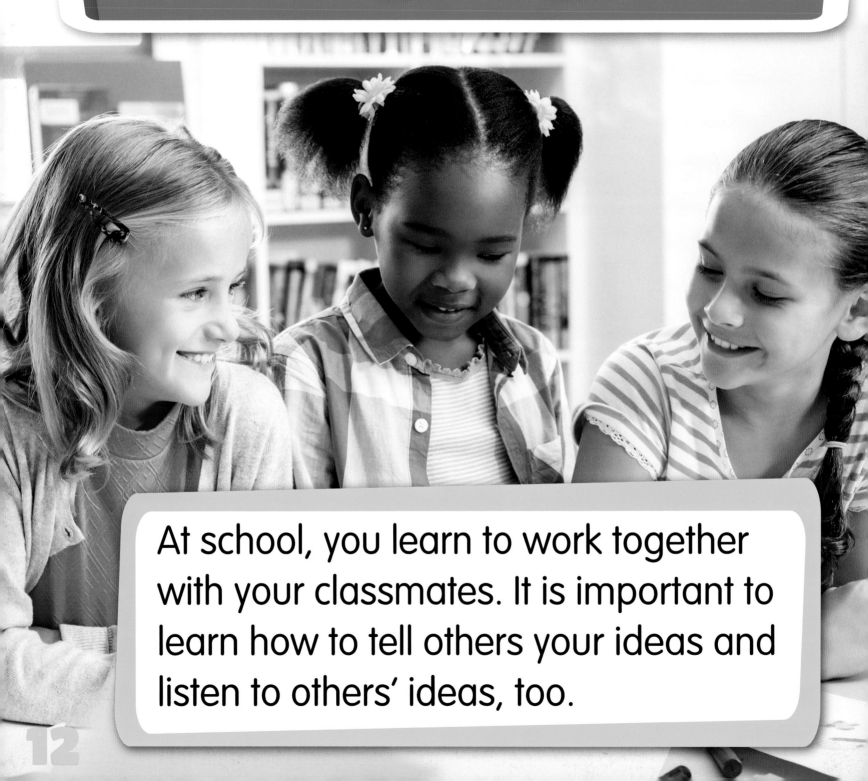

At school, you learn to work together with your classmates. It is important to learn how to tell others your ideas and listen to others' ideas, too.

You can work together with others on the school playground, too!

You must treat your classmates with **respect**. Speak politely to them and listen to their ideas.

15

School Rules

Rules help us all feel safe and welcome at school.

Rules are instructions that tell us what we are allowed to do. School rules must be followed by everyone who learns and works there.

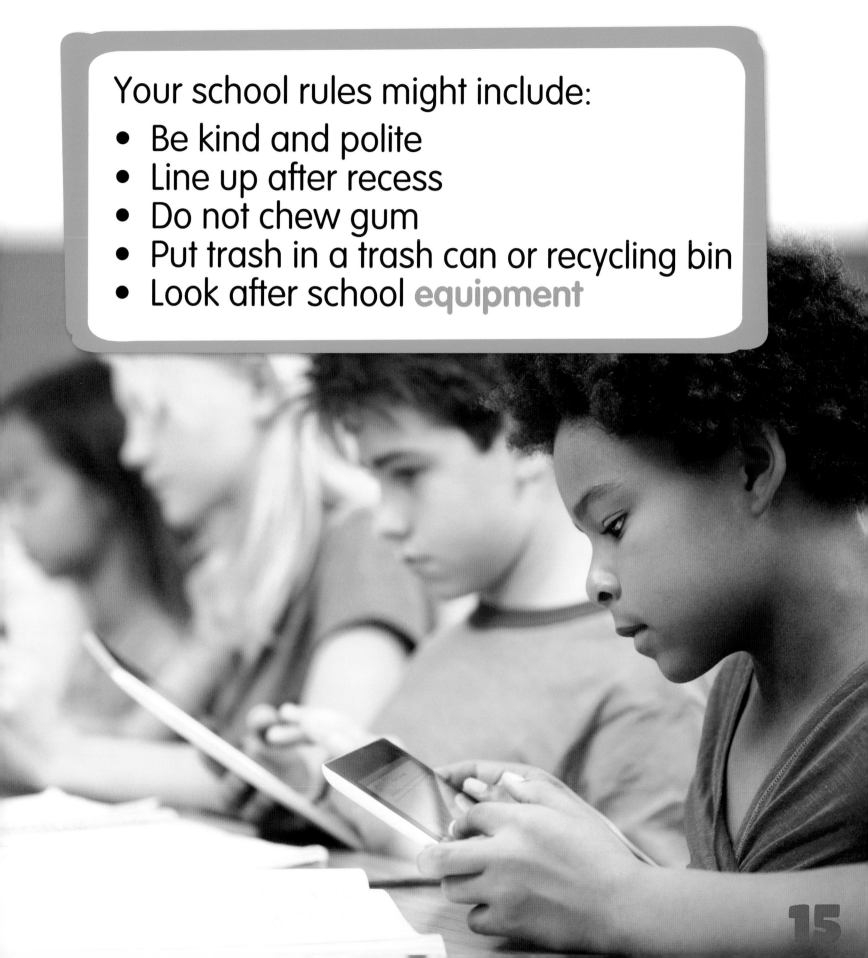

Your school rules might include:
- Be kind and polite
- Line up after recess
- Do not chew gum
- Put trash in a trash can or recycling bin
- Look after school **equipment**

15

Classroom Rules

Class Rules
Listen when someone else is speaking
Work quietly at your desk
Raise your hand when you need help
Treat others with respect
Play Safely - Make wise choices
Respect the person

Classroom rules are often posted on walls.

Classroom rules tell us how to behave in the classroom. They make sure classrooms are good places to learn.

When you follow classroom rules, you are showing respect to your classmates.

Safety at School

These children stay safe on their way to school by wearing helmets and using the crosswalk.

Rules at school and in the classroom can help you stay safe. It is very important to follow them.

Some rules that help you stay safe at school might be:

Do not run in the hallways.

Do not go into a room without a teacher or adult.

Wait your turn to use playground equipment.

19

Doing My Best

Learning can be a lot of fun. But it is not always easy to learn new things. It is important to do your best.

If something is difficult at first, keep trying. Ask your teachers or classmates for help. You can learn from mistakes and try something new next time!

When you keep trying, you can reach your goals!

After School

After school, you might have activities such as music lessons, clubs, or sports. You might have **homework** to do, too.

Each evening, it is a good idea to tell your family members about the things you learned and the activities you tried at school that day.

Glossary

cafeteria	The place in which food is served
community	A group of people who live, work, or play in a place
equipment	Things that are needed for a job or activity, such as helmets for sports
goals	Things that a person wants to do or achieve
homework	School work or activities done at home
respect	Giving someone or something the care or attention it deserves
staff	Workers in a certain place
volunteer	A person who works without being paid

Index